2-17
Lexile: _____

AR/BL: _____3.2_____

AR Points: ___0.5___

Put Beginning Readers on the Right Track with
ALL ABOARD READING™

The All Aboard Reading series is especially for beginning readers. Written by noted authors and illustrated in full color, these are books that children really and truly *want* to read—books to excite their imagination, tickle their funny bone, expand their interests, and support their feelings. With four different reading levels, All Aboard Reading lets you choose which books are most appropriate for your children and their growing abilities.

Picture Readers—for Ages 3 to 6
Picture Readers have super-simple texts, with many nouns appearing as rebus pictures. At the end of each book are 24 flash cards—on one side is the rebus picture; on the other side is the written-out word.

Level 1—for Preschool through First-Grade Children
Level 1 books have very few lines per page, very large type, easy words, lots of repetition, and pictures with visual "cues" to help children figure out the words on the page.

Level 2—for First-Grade to Third-Grade Children
Level 2 books are printed in slightly smaller type than Level 1 books. The stories are more complex, but there is still lots of repetition in the text, and many pictures. The sentences are quite simple and are broken up into short lines to make reading easier.

Level 3—for Second-Grade through Third-Grade Children
Level 3 books have considerably longer texts, harder words, and more complicated sentences.

All Aboard for happy reading!

Library of Congress Cataloging-in-Publication data is available.

ISBN 0-448-42081-3 (GB)   A B C D E F G H I J
ISBN 0-448-42029-5 (pbk.)   A B C D E F G H I J

ALL
ABOARD
READING™

Level 2
Grades 1-3

EGYPTIAN
GODS AND GODDESSES

By Henry Barker
Illustrated by Jeff Crosby

Grosset & Dunlap • New York

It is more than 3,000 years ago in Egypt.

There is a festival in honor of Horus.

Horus was the king of the gods.

The people of ancient Egypt
prayed to many gods.
There were more
than a thousand.

Some looked like
animals.

Some looked like
people.

Some had the head of an animal

and the body of a person.

Each one had special powers.

Re brought the warmth of the sun.

Because of Thoth,
there was the light
of the moon.

Montu guarded warriors
in battle.

All these gods
protected life on earth.

Other gods ruled

the Land of the Dead—

Osiris, Isis, and Anubis.

They were very powerful.

The Egyptians believed
that after a person died,
his soul went to the Underworld.

There were many dangers

on the way.

There were snakes.

There were lakes of fire.

There were demons.

So there were special rules
to travel there safely.

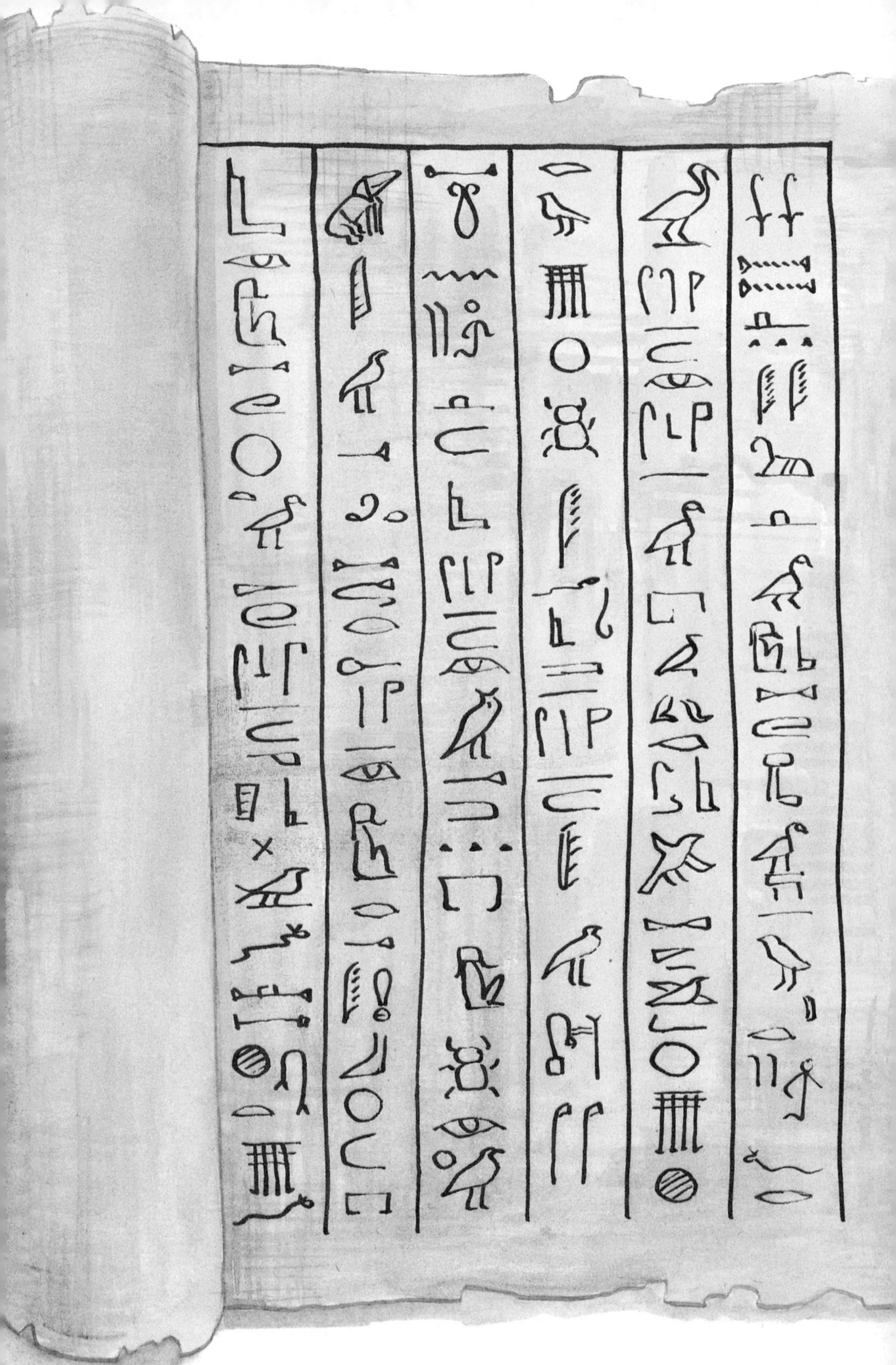

The dead person used magic spells,

prayers, and maps.

The spells came from "The Book of the Dead."

It helped the person get

to the Hall of Judgment.

There, Osiris,

the ruler of the Underworld,

greeted the dead person.

The person had to swear
that his life had been good.
Osiris asked many questions.

If the person's answers
pleased the gods,
then came
the most important test.

It was the Weighing of the Heart.

Anubis held up a scale.

A goddess named Maat placed

her Feather of Truth

on one side of the scale.

She placed the dead person's heart

on the other side.

The gods watched carefully.

A monster with the head of a crocodile

sat close to the scale.

Did the feather and the heart
weigh the same?
If they did, it meant the dead person
had been good.

So the person would go

to a beautiful place—

the Field of Reeds.

Like a god, he would live forever.

But what if the heart

was heavier than the feather?

That meant the dead

person had been bad.

Then the crocodile monster

would eat the heart

with her sharp teeth!

No one wanted that to happen.

All Egyptians wanted to enjoy

a wonderful afterlife.

And it took more than being good.

The soul needed

a body to come "home" to.

So they learned how to keep

a dead body from rotting away.

They learned how to make mummies.

Making a mummy took a long time.

Priests in special masks

helped with the work.

First the organs were taken

out of the body.

Then the body was put

in special salt.

The salt dried out the body.

This took forty days.

After that came a coating of oil and wax.

Finally, the body was stuffed

with cloth or sand

and wrapped in linen strips.

The organs were put in special jars.

The ancient Egyptians became

very good at making mummies.

Some have lasted

for thousands of years.

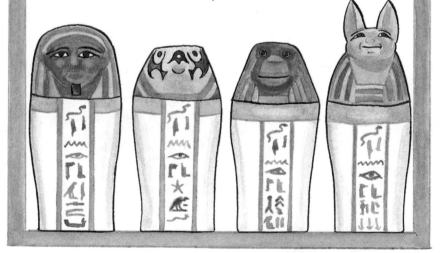

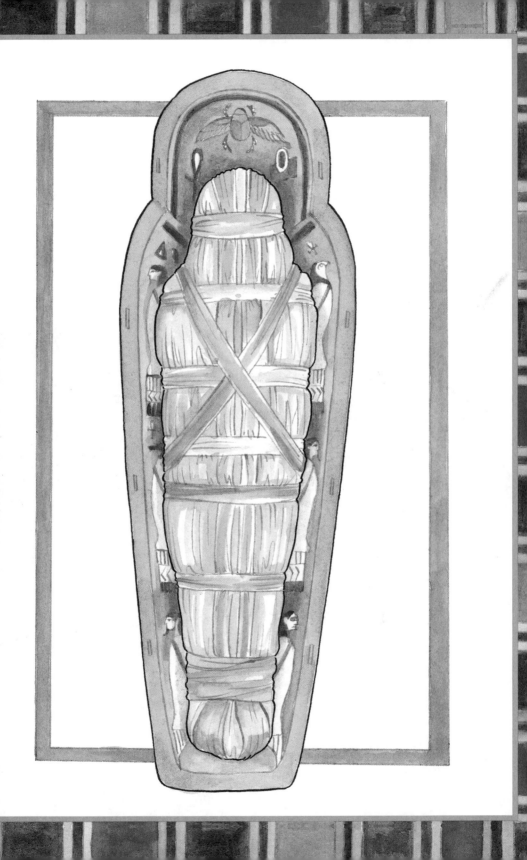

The Egyptians also thought

that mummies had to have special houses.

So they built tombs for them.

They built all kinds.

Some were small—

just holes in the ground.

Others were huge.

Three of the biggest tombs

are still standing.

They are called

the Great Pyramids.

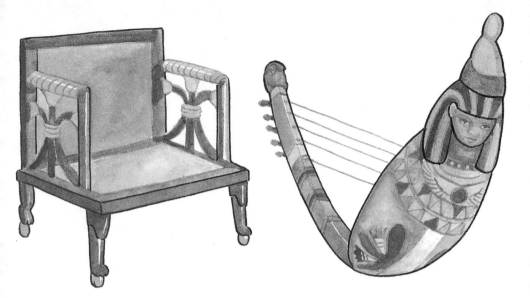

Rich Egyptians wanted
to enjoy their afterlife.
They wanted it to be
like their life on earth.
So they had their tombs
filled with food, jewelry,
furniture, games, and
musical instruments.

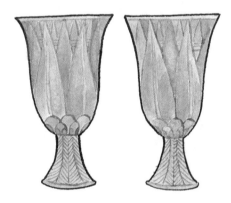

Statues of workers and servants

went into the tombs, too.

The Egyptians believed

that the statues would come to life

and work for the dead person.

Some tombs even had animal mummies.

They had been the pets
of the dead person.

Do people in Egypt
still believe in the old gods?
Do they still make mummies?
No. Their religion changed
long, long ago.

Today most Egyptians are Muslims.

They no longer pray to

Horus or Osiris or Isis.

They pray to one god—Allah.

But every year
thousands of people
visit the ancient temples.
There they see
the old gods,
frozen in time.

Have the old gods lost their power?

Perhaps.

But they will never be forgotten.